EVERYTHING

BRILLIANT

Everything
BRILLIANT

POEMS

Connie Assadi

STILLGROVE

PRESS

Stillgrove Press
P.O. Box 744
Cedar Hill, TX 75106-0744
stillgrovepress@gmail.com

ISBN: 978-1-7332870-0-5 (paperback)
ISBN: 978-1-7332870-1-2 (ebook)

Library of Congress Control Number: 2020901194

Book design and composition by Rachael Brandenburg
Cover design by Rachael Brandenburg
eBook design by Brian Phillips

Editing by April Ossmann
Proofreading by Kim Bookless

Cover photo: OGphoto, iStock by Getty Images
Antique botanical illustrations: ibusca, iStock by Getty Images

First Edition

Published in Cedar Hill, Texas USA

for loved ones
of the three times

CONTENTS

III

IV

V

Preface

The poems in this book arose from the depths of a life-long meditation practice. Over the years, the many insights arising from that practice, some initially painful and worldview shattering, became the impetus behind this sharing.

I have found that the epiphanies life inevitably offers us are elucidated by uncommon moments of clarity in the meditative state. The value of this sharpened perception is inestimable. I suspect I have missed many more opportunities for enlightened perception than I have seized, yet what I've managed to grasp has been life changing. A sustained and devoted meditation practice picks you up exactly where you are and then sets you back down in the very same place with heightened senses to *feel* it, new eyes to *see* it, new ears to *hear* it.

It is my hope some of these poems may sing to you in familiar ways, or better yet, spark remembrance of a splendid song you may have long forgotten.

Is the rising light daybreak,
or the reflection of your face?

—BIBI HAYATI
Nineteenth-century Persian poet

I

ABOUT THINGS

Consider
a wisp of a thing,
insubstantial as a cobweb
billowing in the morning breeze,
hardly even that—

the thinnest veil wafting between
what a thing is
and what we think it is.

Every creature, every rock,
every forest and sea, every mortal
born on this teeming planet,
the luminous moon and all
beyond and below it,

all great mysteries—
yet, it's not the seemingly concrete,
but our thoughts about each thing
which shape our reality.

You may think
you don't know a thing,
but you know it inexplicably,
as your feet know
where the stairs are
in the dark.

SIGNIFICANTLY INSIGNIFICANT

I live beneath the stars, infinitesimal,
a dust mote in this vast universe

of countless expanding galaxies,
invisible dark matter rushing

faster than the speed of light,
and gorgeous paradox:

my smallest move—
a few harsh or kind words

to a store clerk, who carries
their tone home to his family,

an outstretched hand, intended
to help or gesture impatiently,

my turning away
from one relationship

in anger, or toward another
in adoration, the consequences

of my every calculated decision,
or impulsive action—like waves

re-shaping shores—microcosmic
in ways I shall never comprehend,

endlessly revising
the story of the cosmos.

UNMOORED

No anchors or tethers
keep me moored;
I could disappear
into the horizon tonight.

I don't recall how
I arrived in this port, or what
I was supposed to do here.

This eventide,
the sea swallows the sun
in one bright orange gulp,

while eternal questions
bob like foraging sea otters
in the crosscurrent
of all possibility, resurfacing
after each submerging wave.

My small vessel
sails past, gliding across the bay
into uncharted waters,

steered by an unforeseen faith,
captained by a power
greater than my own.

FUGUE STATE

When asked to tell others
something of myself,
I suffer a loss of equilibrium
akin to amnesia.

You might wonder why
an earnest request for introduction
causes such a slip of composure.

A name, an address,
career and family particulars—
such unsatisfying details
form our standard summaries.

How shallow the descriptors
we use to identify
what is steeped in mystery!

Magnificent humans:
walking breathing enigmas,
deigning to give simple answers
to inherently unanswerable questions,

not out of dishonesty, but kindness,
a ruse, so as not to alarm each other
with the truth:

We do not know who we are.

A SECOND LOOK

Old couples
slurping coffee together,
eyes half closed,
always made me nervous.

I scurried away to run errands,
arrive at meetings on time,
finish everything on the to-do list
with diligence, oblivious
to the obvious location in time
of my one irreplaceable life.

Today, sipping from a brimming cup,
I like to think myself wiser.
Even so, I often quite foolishly opt
for a sprint to the future,
over a leisurely stroll through now,
when I can plainly see
the coffee running off his chin
is only

   coffee
     running
      off
     his
  chin,

and a smile can change its course.

THIS CLUMSY STUMBLING

In reverie, it is easy
to see myself
quite outside myself—

as a fallible character
in a tale of pilgrimage
and redemption:

Brash as only youth can be,
she set out—
heedless of slippery stones
or treacherous steepness,
certain of progress.

As the passage grew arduous,
stumbling over roots,
gathering bruises,
feet sore and blisters raw,

who could blame her
for standing motionless and hopeless
beneath winter's sullen clouds, so thick
they obscured the ever-present sun.

When the path appears so does the pilgrim,
yet she finds the road signs
difficult to see in the haze,
or written in a language
she doesn't yet understand.

Hesitation and excessive deliberation
hinder her progress,
as a moonless night hides a trail.

Oh, if only she knew—
even with all this clumsy stumbling,
her destination has always been assured.

THE ILLUSION OF A
PERFECT RELATIONSHIP

How can I bridge this chasm,
rescue us from the dividing darkness
of cold misunderstanding?

Great books have come
and gone from these hands,
yet the right words,
even the simplest mollifying gestures
escape me, taunting as they leave.

The ideal of perfection
turns us inside out, exposing
the festering entanglements
of our attachments and aversions,

like the sight of a rotting tree despoils
the yard, stealing attention
from the colorful daylilies,
honeysuckle and reliable boxwood.

Why can't we see our garden
is lovely enough as it is,
in all its nuanced disparity?

SORROW

Sorrow visits mostly at night;
we hear her weeping
in the stillness,

the soft padding
of her footsteps in the hall,
seeking solace.

In daylight,
she keeps to the shadows
as we perform our chores,
awaiting the least sign—
even the faintest sigh.

I have learned this
about Sorrow:
She needs only to be seen,
and occasionally embraced.

Taken everywhere out of guilt,
she will feel patronized,
and make your life miserable

out of spite, but her sternness hides
a soft side; her pain may be eased
if we invite her sister, Joy,
to spend some time with us.

DEEP IS THE HUNGER

To have or not to have—
that is the question,
once Hamlet's first has been settled,
if only temporally.

So deep is the hunger,
so pervasive the misunderstanding
of why it occurs.

In collecting the finite, we crave
what is infinite, and already includes it.

Aside from bare necessity,
we do not need any gift,
beyond seeing the wealth
in what we have.

ESCAPE

Shhhh . . .
I have somehow wriggled
out of my shackles,
and am sneaking past the sentries.
One creaky floorboard,
and I am toast!

I slip past Doubt
without a sound.
Lucky for me,
she's lost in thought, as usual.

I tiptoe by Fear,
as she takes
a rare afternoon nap.

Resistance is quite busy,
making a long list of reasons why not,
she doesn't notice my passing shadow,
as I sidle out the door.

PRAISE AND BLAME

Like insecure lovers,
Praise and Blame go everywhere together.

Blame, a sneaky chap, lags behind;
to unpracticed eyes, it seems
they travel solo, yet in reality,

Praise knows Blame follows closely,
muttering accusations,
pointing his bony fingers.

Though she is classically beautiful,
wears the latest fashion,
attracts admirers wherever she goes,
Praise always feels uneasy; she knows

Blame boasts fervent devotees—
a rowdy bunch
with chips on their shoulders
and stones in their hands.

He doesn't travel with Praise
so much as stalks her—
not by design or evil intent,
but foolish habit.

VIEW FROM THE SUMMIT

I don't know
if this happens with everyone,
I am not yet that wise in my seeing.

Shadows continue to obscure
realities easily seen by masters.

But some fortuitous glitch
in your ego's clever mechanics
affords me an exceptional view
of your true self.

So, may I say,
from the summit of my own,
how beautiful it is?

II

LOVE IN THIS PLACE

If you leave this planet
having only fathomed Love,
it would be enough.

Such an accomplishment
shouldn't be underestimated
in this world,
where against all odds,
poetry was born—

where Love must get feisty,
demand her due, destined

never to rest on her laurels;
strength to survive tested daily,
shoulder to the sacred stone.

Every morning,
renewed allegiance:

feet to ground
ears to heart
mind open
breath mindful
eyes softened
hands ready
spirit willing

THE STATE OF RHETORIC

In time

nothing is never nothing
everything is also never nothing

never is never *never*
always is never *always*
nor is forever ever that.

A confusing state of rhetoric
until such time

as we are out of time

and the point
of all such argument
is moot.

STRAWBERRIES

Who is to say
strawberries don't taste to you
like carrots or bread do to me?

What is it like for you to experience me?
I only know how you seem
to me—what strange, varying emotions
you evoke moment to moment.

Touching you, I perceive
a sweet sensation, but what of yours?
How can I come to a verdict
hearing only half the testimony?

Together, but still alone, we taste
the fruits of our experience,
as sweet or bitter or sour—
but juice drips from both our chins.

That is the curious fact of existence,
as well as its crazy enchantment.

THE FUTILITY OF
RESISTING LIBERATION

Regarding our homes—
you know the structures I mean,

elaborately constructed out of *woulds*,
shoulds, and *coulds*, keeping us
safely self-incarcerated,

where every pestilent onslaught,
rusting custom or rotting thought
is met with clever justification,
ingenious accusations,

a shrewd use of verbal grout
to keep the shelter intact—

as we strive for control,
because the thought of not knowing
what comes next terrifies,

and though our homes
are just smoldering now, flames
contained to one room, soaked towels
wedged under the door—
they are surely burning down.

We huddle together
on our lonely planet, exposed
to the winds of the universe,
whether we know it or not.

No real certainty
of who we are
or where we are
or what comes next.

Free at last.

JOURNEY FROM HERE TO HERE

Whatever brought this calm,
this tranquil sea of observation,
was an eon coming,
but it could have come swiftly
as a gull swooping to pluck dinner
from Earth's generous feast.

Yet the time it took to get here
is unimportant.

I remember screeching and flapping
uselessly in gusting winds, deaf and blind
to the laws governing sentient life.

Yet the way I took to get here
is unimportant.

The irony of ego
isn't lost on me.
The path of any one
eventually leads back to the all,
and free thought acquiesces,
in the end,
to none at all.

SCRAMBLE

It goes without saying,
without justification,

without any discernible pattern,
ethos, reason, or reasonable
instruction we can see.

Never one nanosecond of life
exactly the same as the next.

Not one mountain or grotto or sea,
not one slithering serpent, splashing fish,
four-legged creature,
or human remains static.

We scramble to find permanence,
but discover our illusions.

LOVED ONES

Let me remember the futility
of our unfortunate penchant
for catastrophic thinking—

the envisioned death of loved ones
inspiring panic, or denial, leading
to over-eating, drinking or working.

Let me remember,
based on the recent discovery
of my propensity for inaccurate projection,

I've never seen my loves
truly until now.

Let me remember what I learned
in stillness—the mystical truth
and irrefutable science:
everything will vanish.

A one hundred percent probability
our loved ones will be lost
to us, or we to them.

Let me remember
to wrap the pain of such transience
around myself like a glittering shawl,

and dance with my loved ones
while I have the chance.

GRATITUDE OFFERING

for Maezen

Your first words captivated me—
as the harmony
of impeccable placement

in the zen garden reveals
a microcosm of the natural world,
enchanting the wide-eyed visitor—

boulders represent mountains,
pools depict lakes,
grassy patches, meadows;

distracted readers may, for a time,
disregard the lessons of weeds,
dreaming of the perfect garden.

But crabgrass and dandelions
are persistent teachers, time
is a patient gardener, passing
without judgment as I practiced,
and when I finally entered Paradise,
a funny thing happened.

I turned the last page,
closed your book,
and promptly forgot it.

My own garden beckoned,
and my attention easily returned
to the one true place
where we look together
in wonder.

How elegant is plain sight in hindsight!
The conundrum of disparate elements
dissolves in an instant,
when conditions are ripe for seeing.

Built into one,
is the salvation of the other,
and the seamless, vaporous whole appears.

So it is with confidence.
Built into insecurity is the salvation of faith.
Built into faith is the humility
of true seeing.

Deep bows
to those who fervently pray
their words are forgotten—
pulled and discarded like weeds,
in the name of true seeing.

III

IN ESSENCE

You are already brilliant,
regardless of any dull reflections
you glimpse window shopping,
in this marketplace of shadows,
projections and illusions—

but neither you nor anything
must change in essence.
What would you change into?

Though eons turn mountains
to dust, and days turn flowers to soil,
not one molecule ever goes missing,

just as stars implode and explode,
in the massive reaches
of this incomprehensible universe, yet
no matter is ever lost.

We can see who we are,
or more obviously are not,

once we have looked earnestly,
and seen
the unabashed sincerity of everything.

THE NEXT RIGHT THING TO SAY

Say it,
for the things we don't say,
we must carry,
heavy baggage
on the road to eternity.

I don't know heaven and angels,
any religion's deities,
or where my winding road leads,

but I do know:
when I slow down,
and gaze at the night sky,

when I wrap myself
in the comforter of silence,
and listen attentively,

I can hear,
whispered on a breeze,
the next right thing to say:

You are loved.

SILENCE AND SPEECH

Silence and Speech
were constant companions, destined
to be at cross-purposes.

Silence accepted all that arose
without discrimination;

Speech insisted on ceaseless comparisons
and tedious analysis, never arriving
at satisfactory conclusions—

when frustration sent her
to Silence for refuge, she felt
annoyance at her inaction.

Speech was capable of sublime heights
in the world of words;
Silence went nowhere
but lived everywhere,
never openly flaunted her beauty,
nor tried to control,
just waited for her friend to see.

Speech needed Silence
for her words to be heard,

Silence needed Speech
to bridge worlds.

No miracle occurred,
just the usual paradox:
when attempts to control
were exhausted by Speech,

Silence clearly spoke her truth
without words,
and Speech heard the truth
within the silence.

SWEPT UP

I know how you love;
I have loved like that.

Such love arranges each particular
to suit personal preference—
the trendiest community
in the most vibrant city,
happy companions, nodding agreement.

A home warm in winter,
cool in summer, windows open,
breeze ruffling the drapery,
too expensive, but so lovely—
what's one more charge on the credit card?

Anyone could see how love
should thrive in such a setting.

I know how you hate;
I have hated like that.

Such hate disguises rationalization
as reason, to suit personal preference—
taking the wrong job in the wrong place,
a lifestyle far beneath fair expectation,
distasteful companions never in agreement.

Anyone could see how such a life
is unacceptable.

How easily we are swept up
in such loving and hating—

hooked on preference
the very first time
we were given a choice,

then carrying on
as if we don't still have one.

As we struggle to live
in the cramped house
of our judgments,

we will come to hate
the conditions we place on love.

Before the mirror
of our hating, if we look
long enough to see through it—

we may come to love
what it reveals at last.

IN TOW

Back in the days
when I did not have the sense
to be suspicious of my longings,

when I strained like a dog on a leash,
could not simply observe
enchanting people or pretty baubles,

but sought to own, to carry home,
to bury hard-won bones in the yard—

in those days
of arched eyebrows,
and games with yardsticks,

it was easy to fall prey
to epidemics of not enough.

Back in those days,
climactic dramas played in the theatre
of my imagination—

every whim grew heavy,
desires came with chains.

But, in tiring of useless tricks,
old dogs, in time, learn useful ones.

Each limiting maneuver guides us,
as a towline restrains a vehicle
but also draws it forward.

APPRENTICE

Beloved poets, dead and alive—
traveling freely through lands
of verbiage; eloquent verse
a passport to spirit zones.

One flight per poet,
no crowding please,
first-class seats available
for the chosen—or so it seemed.

It seemed
holy attributes were allotted
to secret novitiates, trained
in some consecrated place,
anointed with sacred essences
drawn from sacramental wells.

I thought the smell of burnt toast,
a day job crunching numbers,
the vacuum's humming,
the well-worn grooves
of my chronic dissatisfaction,
no probable genesis
for a poet.

Then, to my astonishment,
my apprenticeship began
on a small black cushion—

instrument of my divine discomfort,
unlikely stitched deliverance,
in the spare room's filtered light.

Words rose from wordlessness,
tumbling through sunbeams
of new understandings,
like a sparkling fountain
into a waiting pool.

A grave error to make
too much of them,
or too little.

WHAT WE MISS WHILE WE ARE BUSY

For centuries, humanity has been crammed
into the crowded vestibule of a grand palace,

trying to remember why we're here
and where we're headed,

busy bickering over whose coat
and shoes are whose,

and why my beautiful hat has vanished.
Someone's stolen it, we're sure of that.

He's forgotten galoshes, I regret
my choice of umbrella,

she seeks the perfect scarf
to complement her complexion.

Meanwhile, visible just beyond us
in the Great Hall, a divine fire

blazes in the generous hearth,
revealing in its light,

a long table set for the Feast of Souls,
where wine sits unopened.

In the corner,
a magnificent grandfather clock

ticks stridently,
marking missed opportunities,

awakening us to what we miss
while we are busy;

empty chairs wait
with infinite patience.

UNFORESEEN

In your nightmares,
you were thrown against rocks,
or roamed labyrinthine alleys,
where thieves and monsters menaced;
you saw despair and agony, horrible deaths.

You lost hope, but did not admit this,
even to yourself,
imagining a gossamer thread
as all that wove body and soul together.

Then, an unforeseen day—
the morning's first light
illumines a golden harmony.

It sings to you
from the far reaches of eternity;
it leads you to the sparkling stream
where dry leaves float to the welcoming sea.

Just as fragility meets immensity with grace,
flowing, so you meet your source,
and become in awareness
what you have always been in truth.

THE BIRTH OF PRAYER

You don't have
to learn Sanskrit,
or Hebrew or Latin.

You don't have
to turn beads,
burn incense,
or arrange your hands
this way or that.

After surrender has her way with you—
when the windows finally burst open

from the force
of your sighs,

and a startling lucidity
kicks in the door—suddenly,

prayer is the board,
the vegetables, the knife;

prayer is the blossom,
the breeze, the fragrance.

It is the thought,
and the awareness of thinking,
the dance and the choreography,

the evening's supper
and the greengrocer's stand.

Prayer is the air,
the breathing, and the breath.

It sees the world from your eyes,
tastes fruit with your mouth,
hears music with your ears,
feels love everywhere.

Prayer is born
because of you.

IV

SURVIVAL STRATEGY

By day, place your attention
on the world beneath your feet.

Observe the industry of tiny ants,
lifting, pulling crumbs toward their colony,
in a marvel of skill and cooperation.

Notice nature's treasure trove
of fleshy fruits and diaphanous wildflowers,
verdant meadows and crystalline granite,
spiral shells in turquoise shallows.

Contemplate the oak's unseen roots,
couriers of earth's complimentary
nourishment.

Walk slowly, carefully,
presuming a small misstep could send you
tumbling off the planet.

By night, study the sky,
as if the answers to all life's secrets
were written in code
with the positions of the stars.

Ponder the inadequacy
of the words *eternity* and *endless*,
to describe the immensity
of what cannot be explained
in any language.

Learn the math of the speed of light;
try to wrap your head
around the distance of a light-year.

If you allow your senses
to be astonished, in reverie of the heaven
of worlds above and below,

why would you be disturbed
by anything in between?

CHILD
for Amanda, Paige, and Abraham

Child of mine—
do not be fooled
by my habitual bluster,
seeming reticence,

or any of the many foolish ways
I may try to influence you,
make you in my image,
or live my life through you.

I know better,
in the wholeness of my being,
but I'm wired for maternal radar,
scanning the radio waves
for even the faintest distress signal
by day, and replaying a medley
of my greatest flubs
at night, in lieu of sleep.

I control your life's trajectory
no more than a faulty bow does its arrow—
I make your decisions
no more than I instruct the wind
how hard to blow.

I rest powerless
in my love for you, sobered
by the requisite letting go.

I think you may not believe it,
but in this winter of my life,
I have come to know my shortcomings
almost as well as you do.

I ask for forgiveness—

not for my sake,
but for yours,

and for Forgiveness herself,
who aches to feel
what it is to prevail
in a heartbroken world.

ON ENTERTAINING HOPE

Let's help each other remember,
fellow pilgrim, to let it go—
something, someone, somewhere better—

let it all go, as the moon's dark side
forgoes her light, as the ocean's depths
ignore her heaving surface.

Let's take a nap
and give our egos a rest
from the busy work
of entertaining insatiable hope.

Everything we need is already here;
hope is a door-to-door salesman—
let's ignore the buzzing.

When we awaken refreshed,
when we yawn and stretch,
and look around,
smiles may creep slowly
across our beautiful faces.

We may even laugh
at the absurdity of our discontent,
and that would be a very good sign.

HOW TO LIKE YOURSELF

If you look,
and do not like what you see,
you are not seeing clearly.

Remember to look at what you *are*,
Not at what you *do*.
What you do follows
what you think you are,

what you are
no more follows what you do,
than a horse follows the cart.

EVEN WHEN WE MISS THE POINT, THE POINT REMAINS

Dear moon,
do me a tiny favor, will you?
Please scatter the clouds
obscuring the view
between you and me.

In recompense,
let me be a mirror
of your steady brilliance,
a reminder of your light
when clouds return.

THE NATURE OF ONE

The sage spoke to us of one use
of discipline: hardening the self
to granite, impervious and unassailable.

A few disciples asked him to expound—
the idea of being rock not appealing,
having weathered
their fair share of hardship.

The sage replied with another use:
softening oneself into cloud—
nebulous and fluid, permeable,
then vanishing.

Having been enchanted
by beautiful drifting clouds,
this charming transformation
inspired the disciples to ask
how they might accomplish it.

Easy, said the sage:
to become rock,
use discipline to follow mind,
no matter what.
To become cloud,
use discipline to follow heart,
no matter what.

Debate ensued between disciples
who claimed rock as better,
and those who favored clouds.

The sage smiled,

You are all right.
You are all right as rain.

And rain is the subject
of tomorrow's talk.

THE DILEMMA OF BEING PRESENT

Is there a way to not be here,
but still be here? Sign me up,
the minute I am completely fed up
with reading recipes
in an empty kitchen.

I could write
one hundred thousand poems
about nothing, and still hanker
for just one morsel of something
to sate my hunger.

I could speak about everything
I never knew, and have said
too much, but not enough.

ALL WILL REVEAL ITSELF

I have rowed my boat
up the river of dreams, I have climbed
lofty mountains from the valleys
of illusion below.

I have passed through canyons
of misery and danced in meadows
of granted wishes.

I have drowned in floods
brought on by storms
of self-indulgent emotion,
blinded by self-made fog.

I have seen, and begged to see,
I have walked right past, and not seen.

I have basked in the pristine light
of the fullness of life,
as it enters my window
through the haze
of my imperfect understanding.

I finally have come to trust
in time, or out of time,
All will reveal itself.

CROSSING THE RUBICON

Dear fellow hiker
in the valley of failure—
wearied by the rugged path,
considering retreat—

don't turn around,
or set your pack down now.

This is your apotheosis,
the fork in the trail
offering freedom
from the concepts grieving you.

Rejoice as you rise each morning
from wandering dreams,
follow the canyon's inclinations,
the winding rock-strewn paths;
you will, in time,
come to a redeeming brook.

There, dear traveler,
you will cross the Rubicon
of your deliverance from self,
and the particulars
of your seemingly solitary existence
will shine with revealing light.

V

ESTRANGEMENT

This poem reaches backward
and forward through time
to bring you an important message.

It seems I have been gone longer
than any remembering,
living in the recesses of your forgetting.

Listen,
you might hear me sigh faintly,
when your resistance
to change shoves you
into some fresh catastrophe,
or otherwise disrupts
your well-ordered life—

when friends turn unexpectedly into foes,
and lovers reject you.

For each downturn of fortune,
unhappy thought,
and deep mire of grief—
I was with you.

I wept constantly
for your needless despair,
shadowed your every move
when you were lost,

hoping you would notice me,
and let me lead you home.

My devotion to you is resolute,
my faith in you complete.

Deep in your cavernous depths,
dear one,
you know it to be true:

your tragic play
has a divine plot twist at the end,
all dire appearances aside.

CLUELESS

After all my time
in a stormy love affair with life,
what do I know?

Laws for everything,
explanations for nothing.

My desire for clarification
obscures
what is closer
than a lover's breath,

but further
than my human eyes
can properly see.

Elucidation offered in dreams
is hard to hold onto; I wake
tangled in my sheets' white flag.

From mystery I came,
in mystery I find solace,
toward mystery I am propelled,
into mystery I will disappear.

FRUITION

To become acquainted with truth,
approach with your half-truths,
offered as rice to a beggar—
no expectation of anything in return.

Your half-truths contain seeds of truth,
will bloom in the ground of your being,
given the steady rain of everyday life,
the nutrients inherent in patience,
and faith's eternal sunlight.

You say the rain is unrelenting,
and the patience, the faith,
have gone missing,

but I see the patience
in every day you rise,
the faith in each step you take—

and the mercy of fruition,
yours for the picking.

ALL YOU WILL EVER NEED

Remember, dear friend,
the drowning grasp at anything.

They will sputter and flail,
then commandeer
your divinely sturdy boat.

You may as well give them the oars,
the life jackets
and the compass too—

until you're alone
in the vast ocean of giving,

until all you have
is what you are.

That is all
you will ever need.

THE END OF ME

What good is this apparition I call *me*?
Best to burn me off like morning fog
or drizzle me all over creation.

Let me softly land, then melt,
like fresh snow on rocky outcroppings.

Let me flow over the open plains,
leaving the wildflowers drenched
and bowing.

Take me and fill each crevice,
patch each fissure
in the earth's untamed wildness,
smooth ground for the journeying masses.

With gossamer strands of me,
weave a soft blanket for covering
those who cry in the night.

Then, with what is left of me,
to each lonely being calling for solace,
searching for an unknown something,
let me be that.

Though in reality they don't need me,
and have only been caught in a web
of imaginary spiders, let me be

the imperceptible wisp of wind
to finally blow it away,

revealing illusion's gauzy trap
to eyes weary of witnessing
the suffering of eons.

DEAREST DEATH

Dearest Death,
a note of apology:

Truth is,
I always shunned you—

peeked out at you,
then slammed the shutters tight.

The day you came to knock
on every door around me,

no longer a presence I could ignore,
I took to studying you.

I saw the grace imbued
in every departure—

gradual,
or wrenchingly swift.

I saw the wisdom
in your resolve, your reliability—

never shirking
your grievous responsibilities.

How you must love us,
to take on such a thankless profession!

A hallowed breeze, your breath
on my neck, such sweet consecration.

All that appears, disappears.
Now, I would not have it any other way.

It is you, dearest Death,
who has brought me full to life.

I'LL SING

In the absence of answers,
lapped by flames of confusion,
from the funnels of darkness,
and up stairways of light,
starting in all places,
ending in none—
I'll sing.

I'll sing you to sleep, I'll sing you awake.
I'll sing your cup full and your tears dry.
I'll sing when all else is silent,
and my anthem, too, will be hushed—
a lullaby for all places and all times.

From discord and despair,
from the guts of the mess
this errant digression has wrought,
a sweet strain, an offering, will sow
heirs of devotion
in the fields of great hunger,
where each stalk
hides a bounty
of seeds.

VESSEL

Every treasured family bowl,
each long-stemmed beauty held aloft
in sweet celebration;

baby's first cup,
lovely pottery shaped on the wheel
by a daughter's own hands,

jars of luscious preserves,
cellared bottles of wine,
every vessel you can name or imagine—

fragile! And to hear eternity tell it,
already emptied, already broken.

Greenware is malleable,
useless until fired.
Likewise, we sentient vessels,
yearning to be filled,
already contain a cleansing flame—

burning to the surface
over seconds or lifetimes,
consuming all our glorious designs,

leaving us with nothing we forged,
but everything brilliant.

THE MYTH OF CREATION

Just as something seems to come
from nothing with a big bang, nothing
seems to come from some things—
a cold dark matter to contemplate.

Or is it all coming apart at the *seems*?

Atoms arrange and rearrange,
molecules bond and part,
nothing's new,
but everything's original.

Artists intuit it well:
what is, is here to see—
the figure within the marble,
the truth within the poem,
the life within the life
of everything in creation.

BEYOND BEYOND

Each lesson and epiphany
sharpens awareness,
like a pristine mountain spring
affords a clear view
of underlying pebbles and stones.

But habits, misperceptions,
and folly, flowing synchronously,
form a stubborn sludge.

My attention wanders to treetops,
takes fanciful flight, till patiently,
I tease it back to this stream,
flowing at my feet, ever-changing,

as my theories of making meaning
rise like mist, only to dissipate
in bright sunlight, or drift away
on currents of restless thought.

Within my exquisite bewilderment
I live like a phantom,
keeping my bags packed—

for any day now,
I may be called to move
beyond any questions,
beyond the idea of moving on,
beyond the notion of beyond.

PARTING WORDS

If I didn't cobble these words
together for you, I'd be remiss
in my contributions.

Yet, I beg of you,
disregard everything—
I have said too much.

I'd rather you watch the sky
from your front row seat,

invite the wind
on a play date with your hair,

pull loved ones close,
to comfort and to treasure,

forgive a million times,
and give a million more.

Eat an apple.
Drink some tea.
Walk.
Breathe.
Live.

REUNION

Cease, cease!
Do not seek, be sought out.

Hush, hush—
Do not choose, be chosen.

Be still, be very still . . .

In this grove of solitude,
not a leaf rustles, nor a twig cracks.

Everything awaits your return,
frozen with longing.

You have searched for me backwards:
take the inner passage,
I abide within.

I am that quiet voice you ignored,
the wild idea you discounted,
outrageous strength,
sacred tenderness,

the essential beingness you craved
from the time
you took your first big gulp of air,

from the time
you entered this curious labyrinth.

In your confusion and distraction,
you misplaced me.
In all the commotion, you forgot about me.

Yet I wait steadfastly,
thrilled by the approach of our reunion.

Come, come!
The time is now.

Acknowledgments

This book exists because of countless generosities. I especially would like to thank:

My late parents, Shirley and Ron Walker, for their unwavering support and love.

My sister and emotional safe harbor, Rhonda Marshall, who unfailingly offers me comfort in hard times, reality checks when needed, and infectious exuberance in times of good fortune and joy.

My brother, Jeff Walker, for his encouragement of my writing and for keeping me accountable when my feet were dragging by frequently asking the dreaded question: *How's the book coming?*

My children—Amanda, Paige, and Abraham, who have taught me that I can learn from the past as well as lean gently toward the future while my feet are planted firmly in the present.

Author and Zen Buddhist priest Karen Maezen Miller, for her luminous writings, her friendship, and a memorable summer afternoon in her garden.

My editor, accomplished poet, and teacher of poets, April Ossmann, who with impeccable expertise, cheery helpfulness, and stellar tact, adroitly guided me to places of greater clarity and cohesion.

Cindy Manning and all my colleagues at Manning & Associates, for providing the most relaxed and trusting work situation an accountant/wannabe poet could possibly hope for.

Finally, and most importantly, my husband, Mike, who not only cooks us wonderful food and brings fresh-baked bread to my office as an afternoon snack but has steadfastly stuck by my side for decades, through innumerable ups and downs and all arounds. Bonus points for tenacity, honey.

About the Author

Connie Assadi lives in a quiet suburb of Dallas, Texas, in a cozy home with a room that serves both as a home accounting office, where she prepares financial statements for doctors, and poet's lair, where this book was written surreptitiously. How the two occupations happily coexist is a mystery to her.

When not writing verse or crunching numbers, she reads, does laundry, cleans, and makes baked goods she likely should not eat. Her hobbies include bickering with her resolute husband over unimportant things and worrying needlessly about her three grown children, who are perfectly capable and wise beings.

Every day she makes time to sit on a small black cushion and simply breathe.

www.ingramcontent.com/pod-product-compliance
Lightning Source LLC
Chambersburg PA
CBHW021935040426
42448CB00008B/1080